This Book Belongs to:

Coloring Pack
Copyright (c) 2020 all rights reserved

Part 1: Learning Letters

Trace the letters and practice writing them in the remaining space!

Use the blank practice page to write on your own at the end.

A B C D E F G H I J K L M N O P Q R S T U V W X Y Z

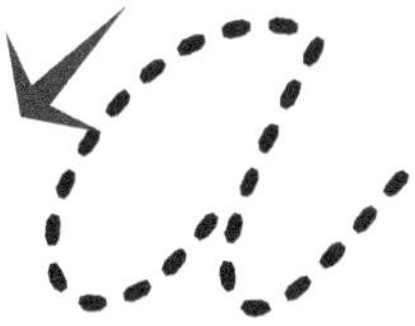

a a a a a a a a a a a

a a a a a a a a a a a

A A A A A A A

A A A A A A A

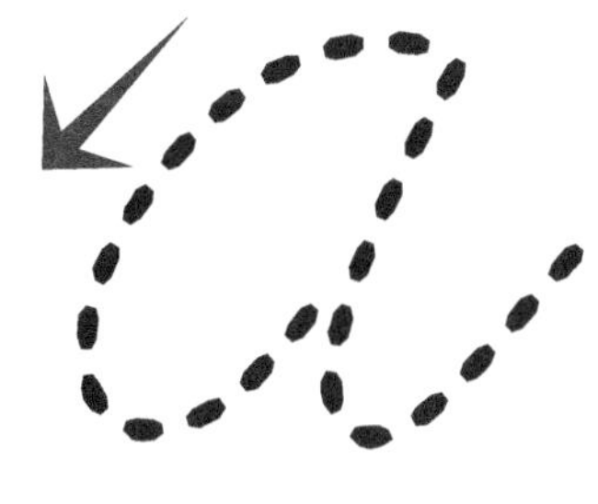

ABCDEFGHIJKLMNOPQRSTUVWXYZ

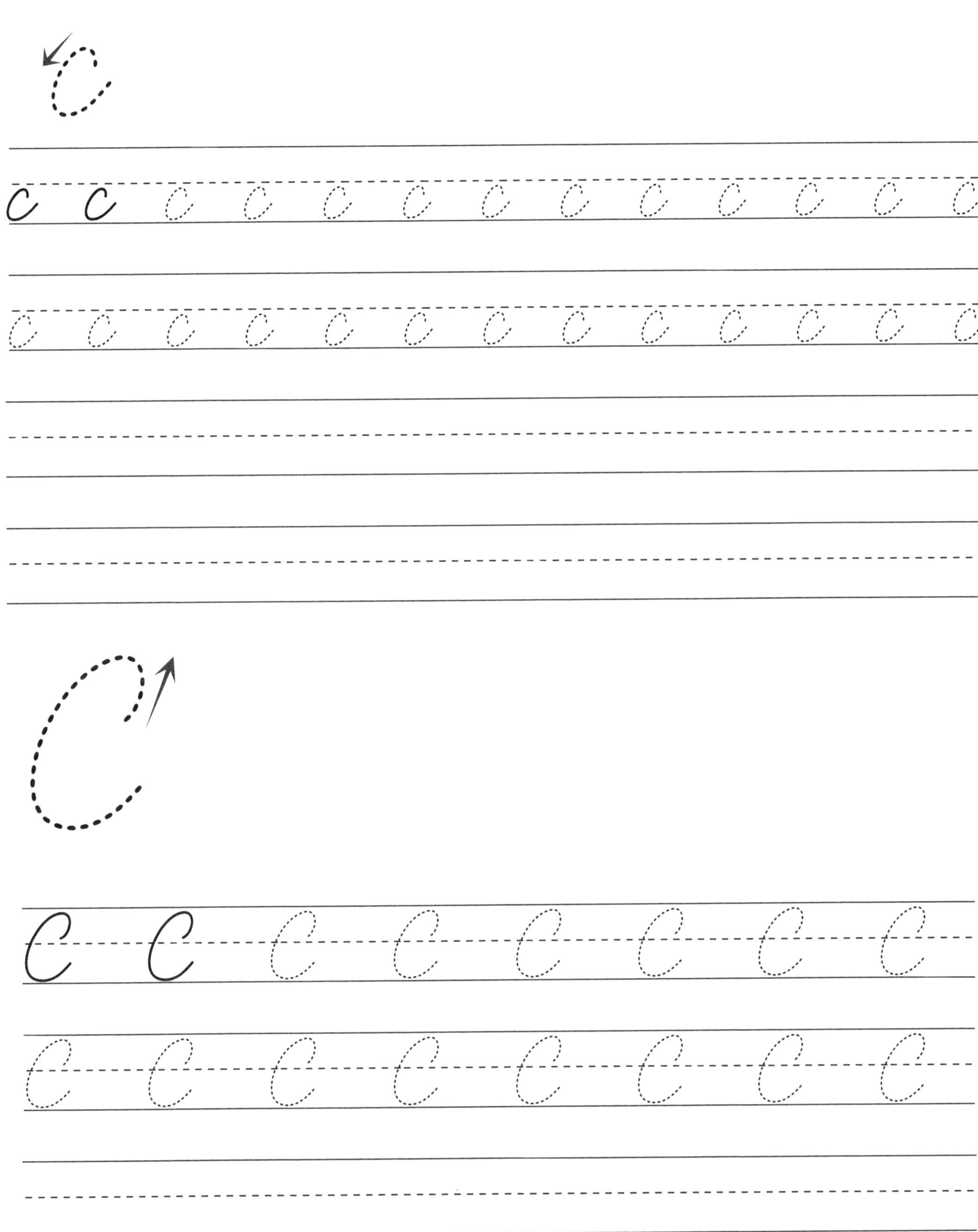

A B C D E F G H I J K L M N O P Q R S T U V W X Y Z

ABC**D**EFGHIJKLMNOPQRSTUVWXYZ

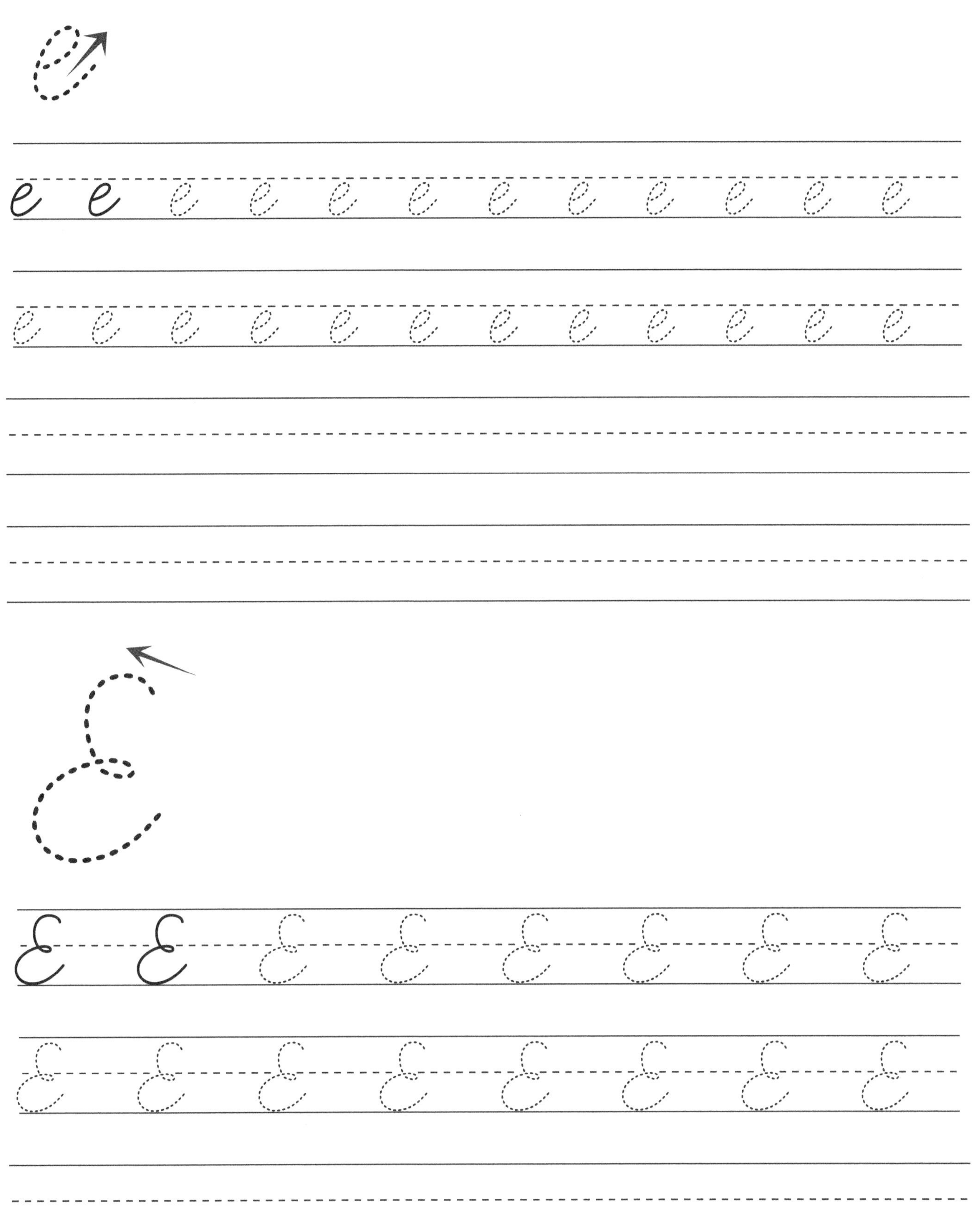

A B C D E F G H I J K L M N O P Q R S T U V W X Y Z

ABCDE F GHIJKLMNOPQRSTUVWXYZ

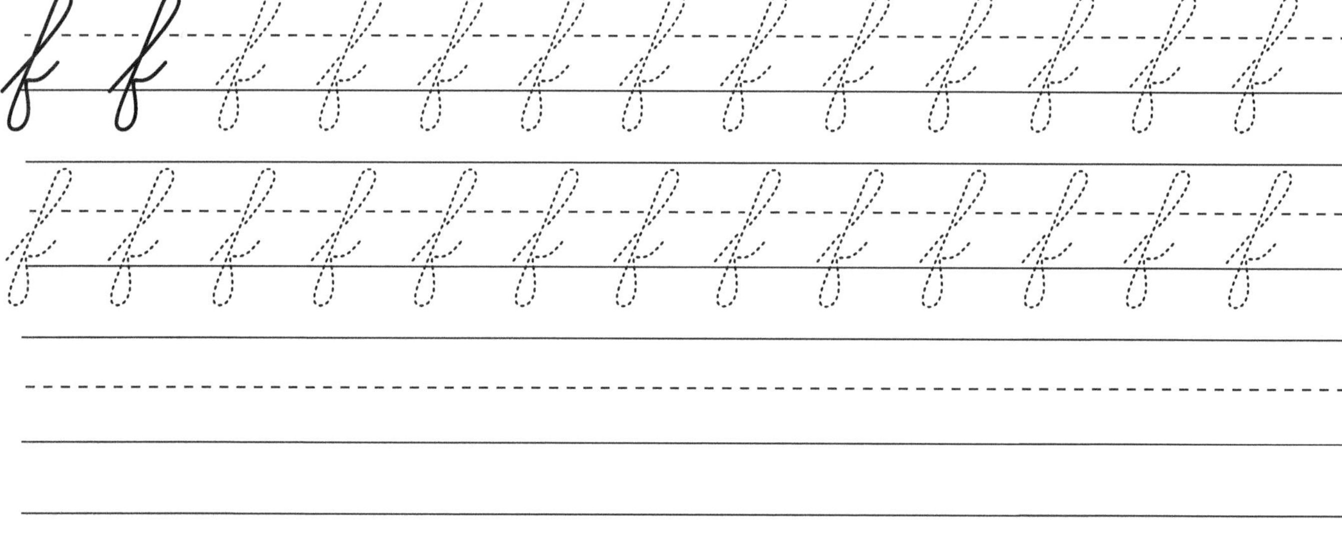

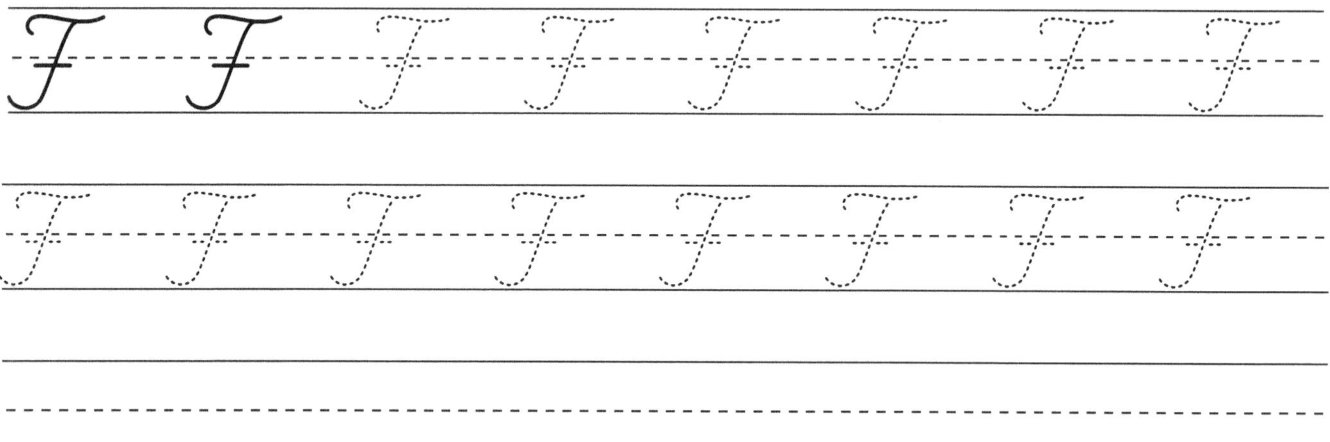

ABCDEFGHIJKLMNOPQRSTUVWXYZ

ABCDEFG**H**IJKLMNOPQRSTUVWXYZ

A B C D E F G H **I** J K L M N O P Q R S T U V W X Y Z

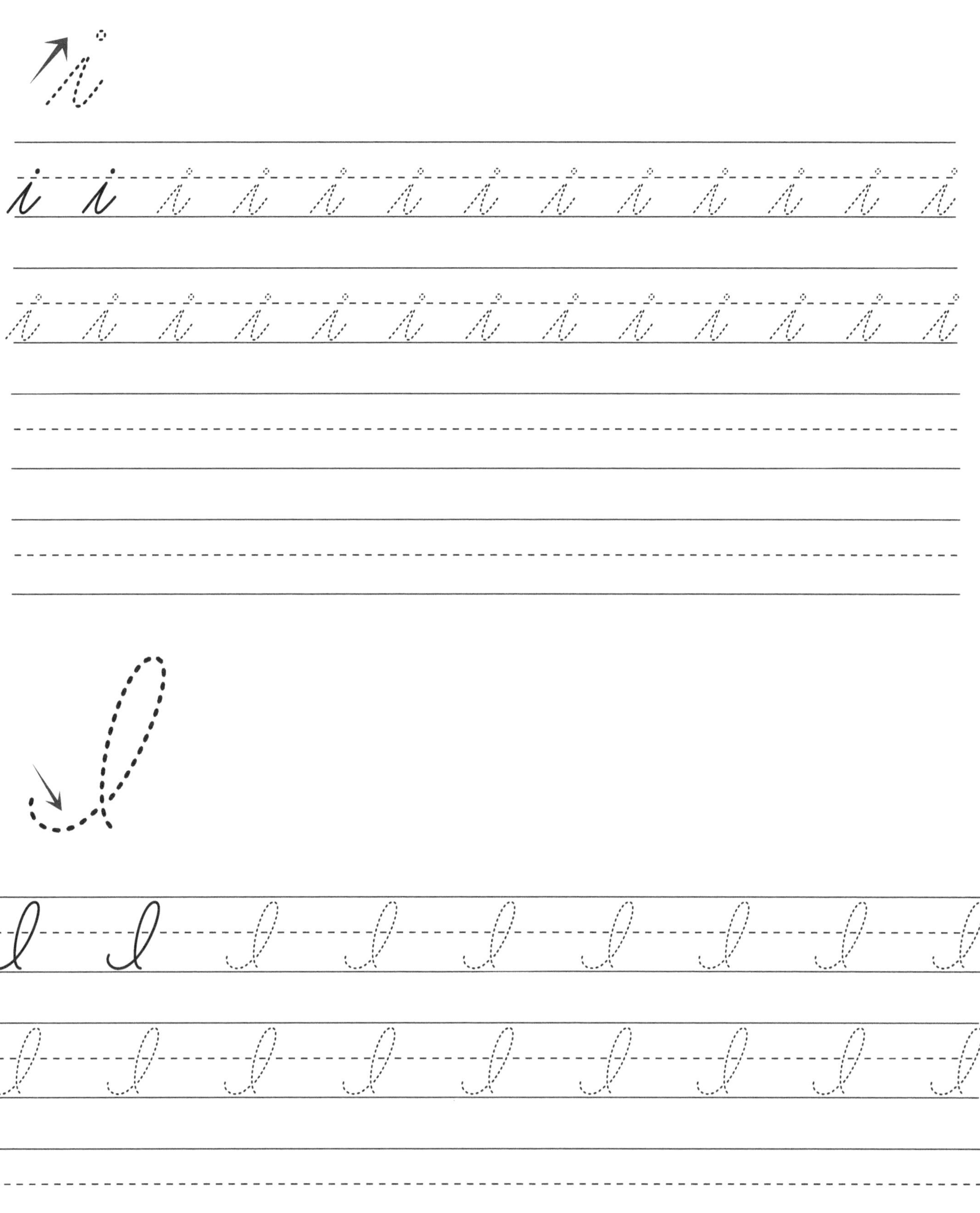

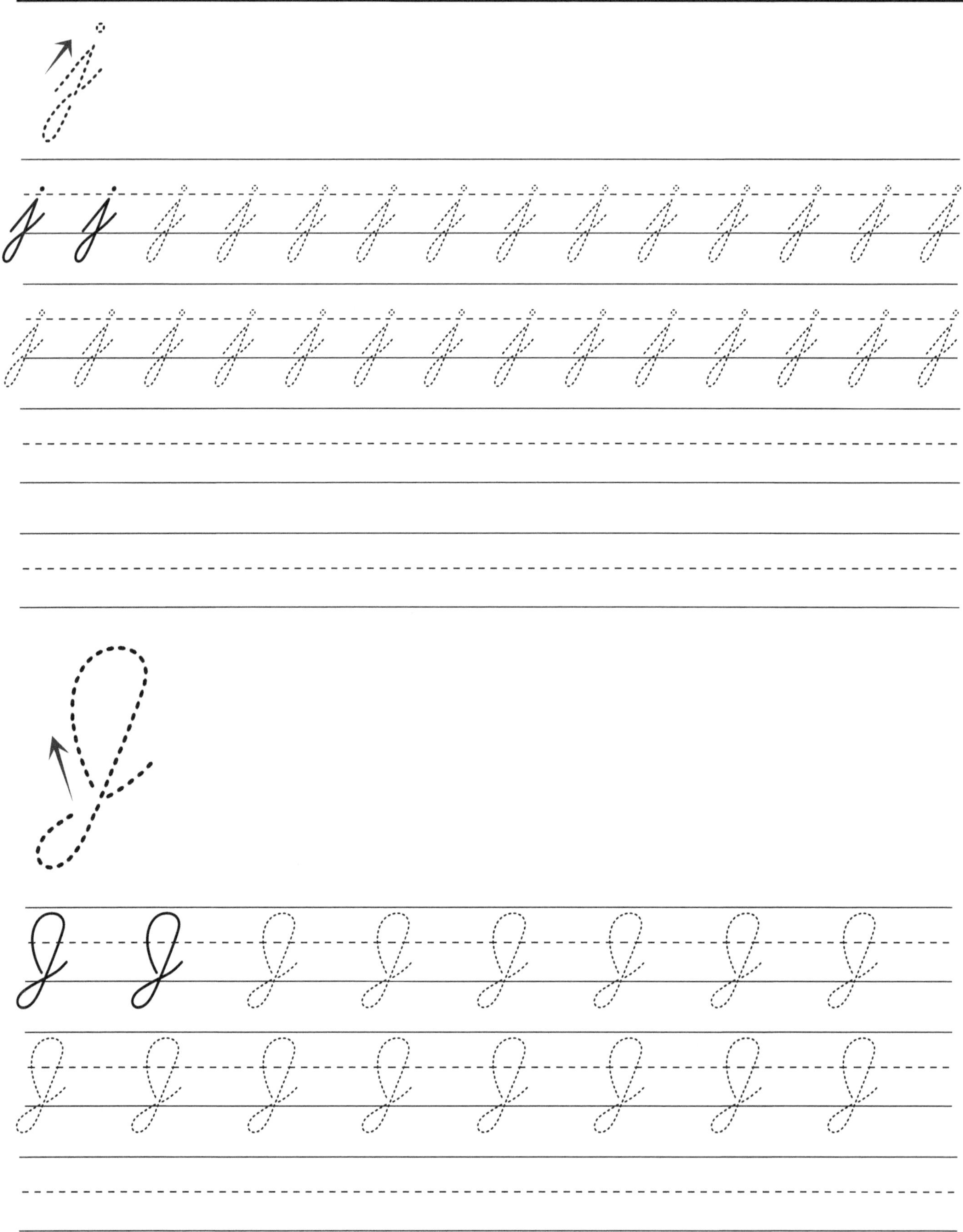

A B C D E F G H I J K L M N O P Q R S T U V W X Y Z

ABCDEFGHIJ[K]LMNOPQRSTUVWXYZ

A B C D E F G H I J K **L** M N O P Q R S T U V W X Y Z

l l

L L

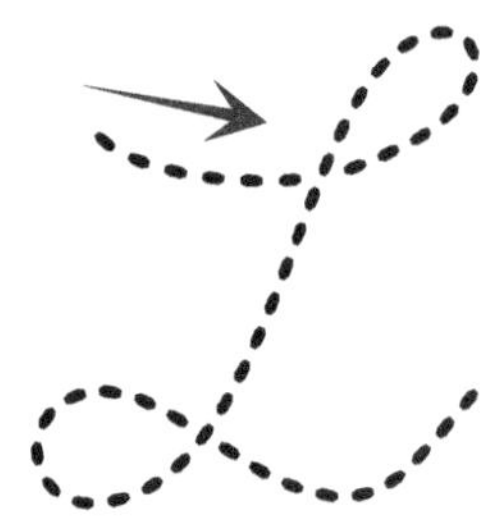

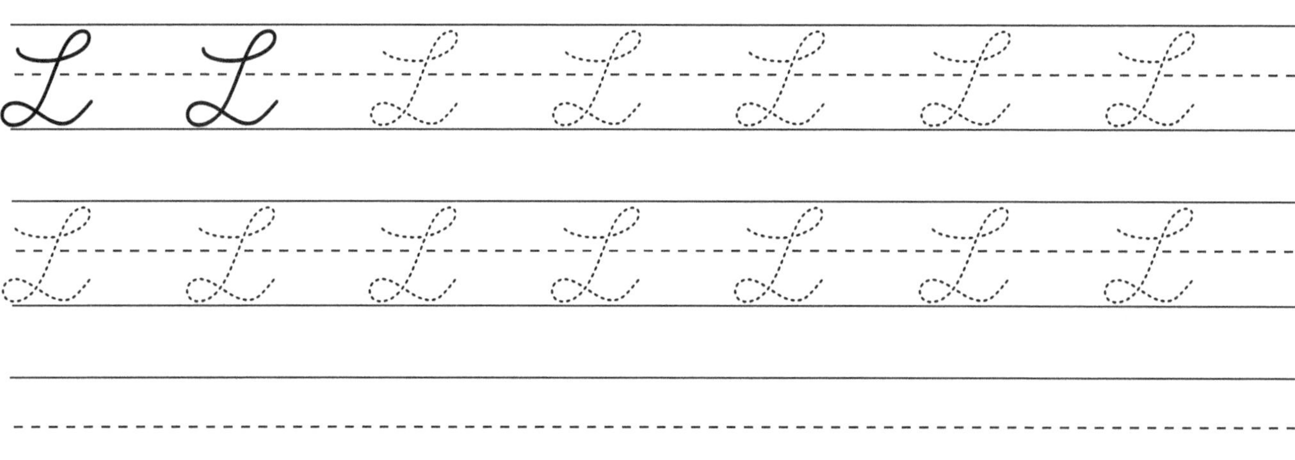

ABCDEFGHIJKL **M** NOPQRSTUVWXYZ

ABCDEFGHIJKLM**N**OPQRSTUVWXYZ

A B C D E F G H I J K L M N O P Q R S T U V W X Y Z

ABCDEFGHIJKLMNO**P**QRSTUVWXYZ

ABCDEFGHIJKLMNOP**Q**RSTUVWXYZ

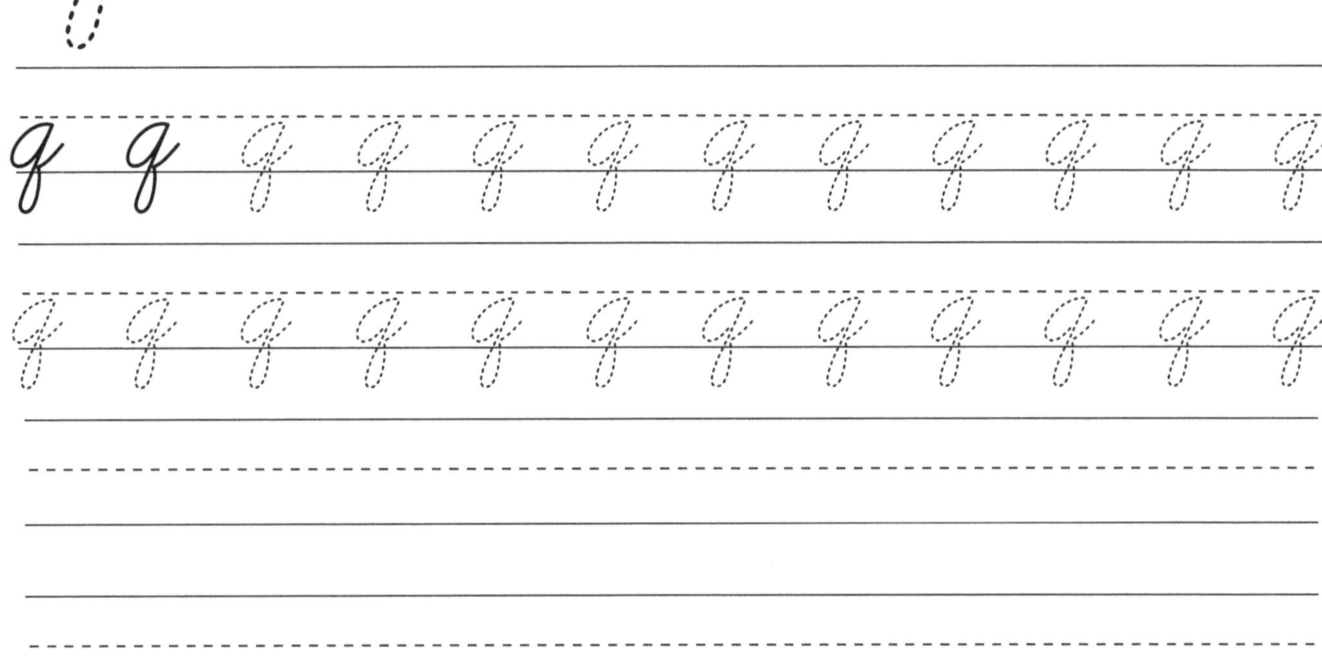

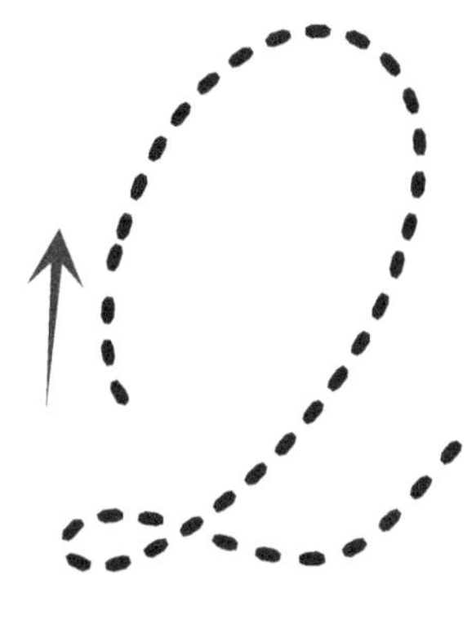

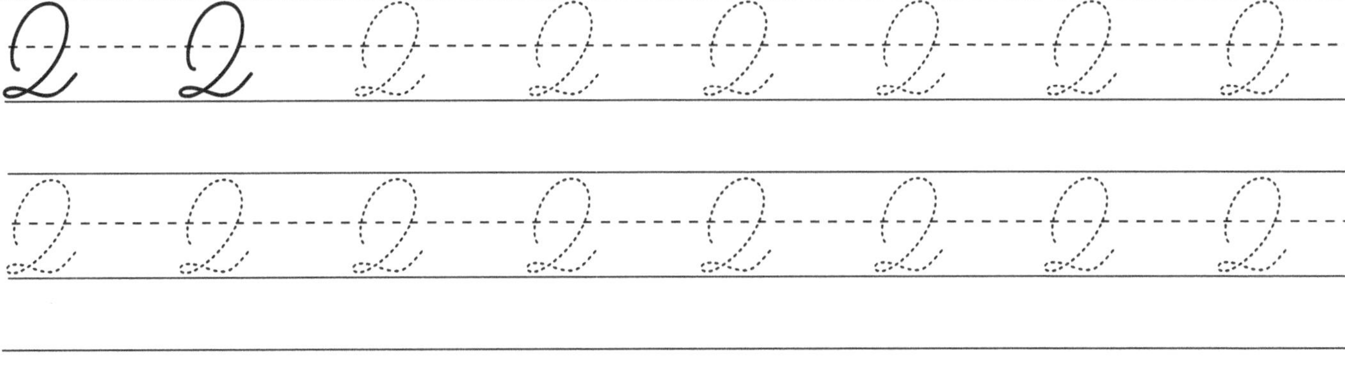

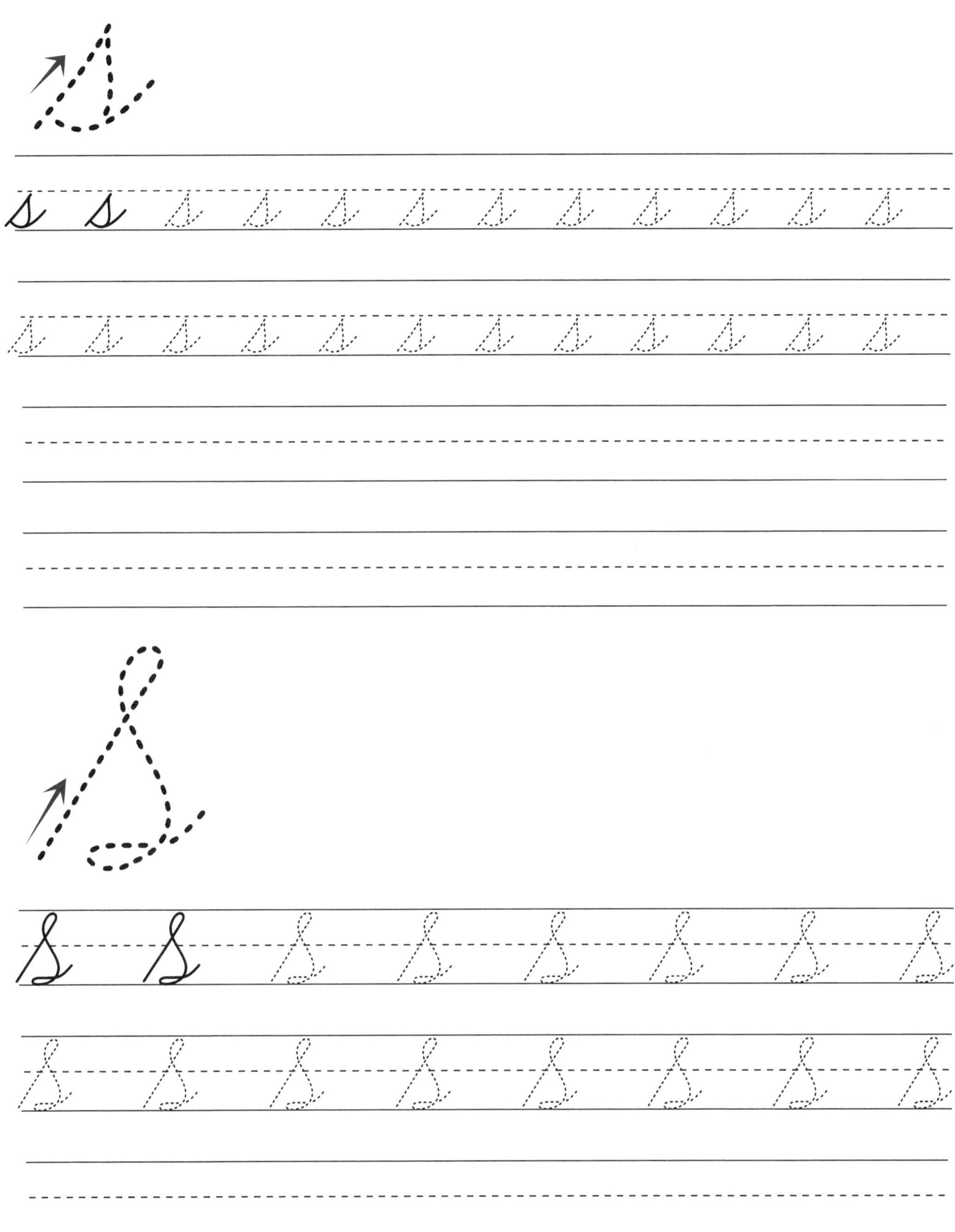

ABCDEFGHIJKLMNOPQR S TUVWXYZ

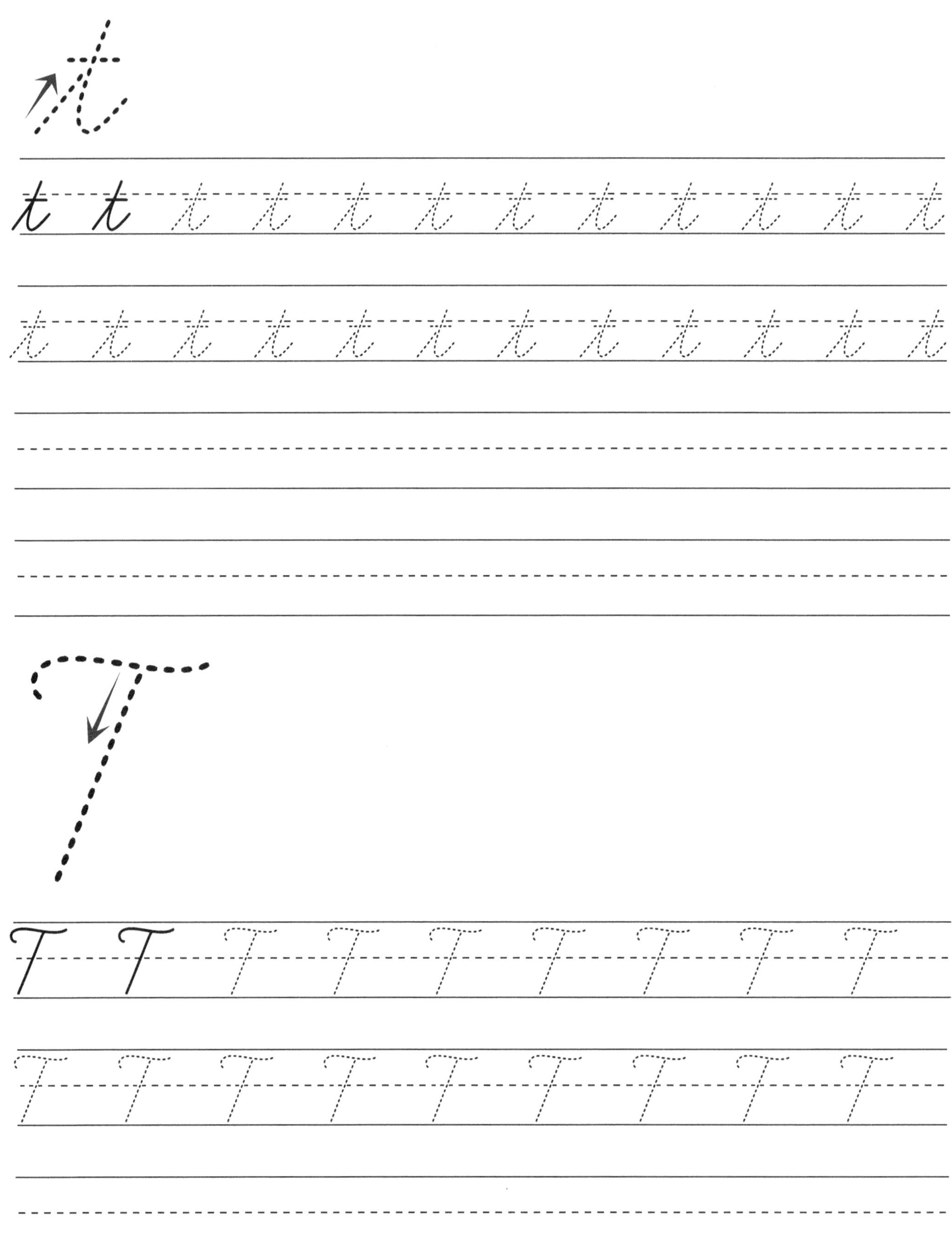

ABCDEFGHIJKLMNOPQRS T UVWXYZ

ABCDEFGHIJKLMNOPQRST**U**VWXYZ

ABCDEFGHIJKLMNOPQRSTUV[W]XYZ

ABCDEFGHIJKLMNOPQRSTUVWXYZ

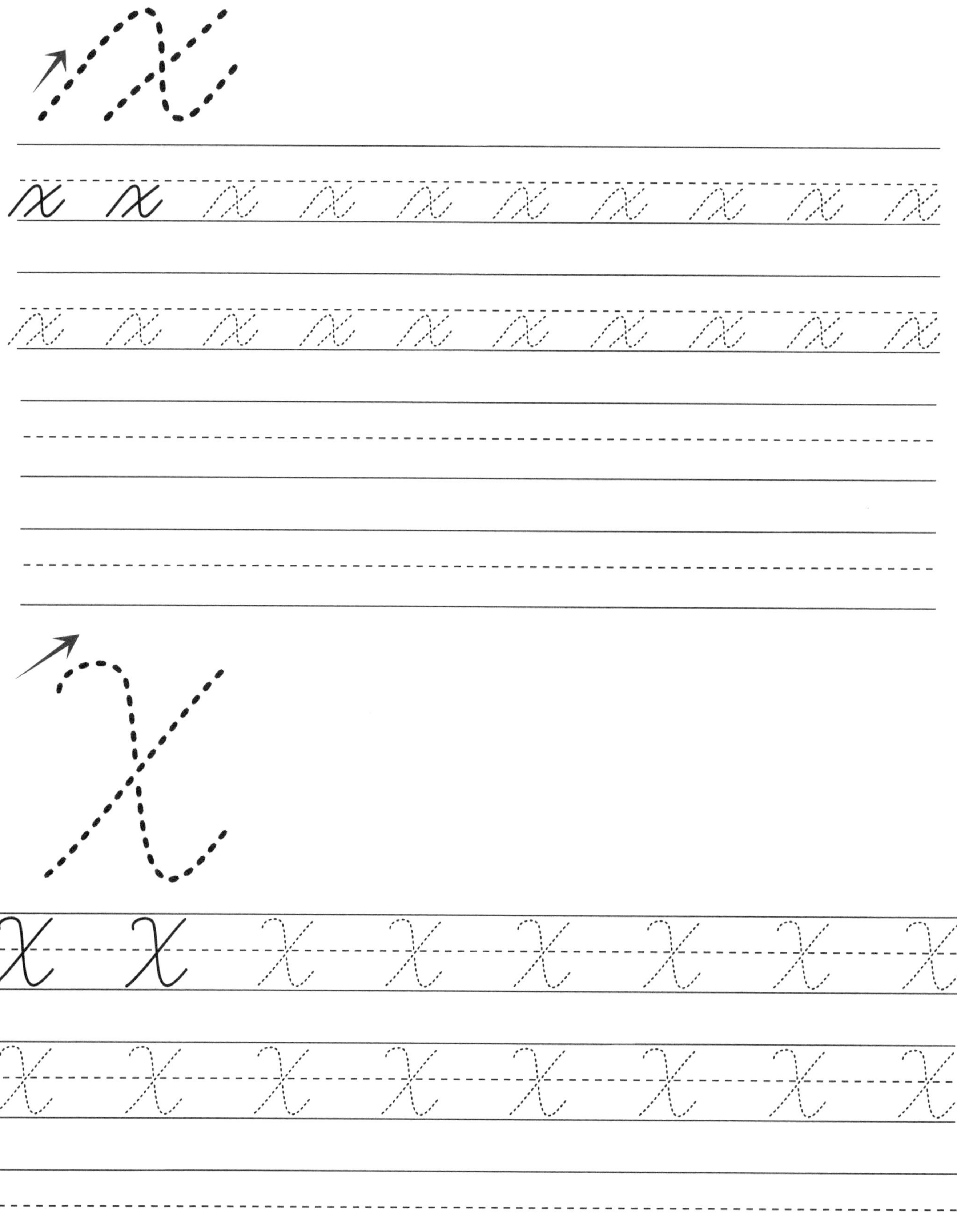

A B C D E F G H I J K L M N O P Q R S T U V W X Y Z

A B C D E F G H I J K L M N O P Q R S T U V W X Y Z

Part 2: Learning Words

Trace the words and practice writing them in the remaining space!

Use the blank practice page to write on your own at the end.

boy *boy boy boy boy*

girl *girl girl girl girl*

boy and girl

baby *baby* *baby* *baby*

kids *kids* *kids* *kids* *kids*

baby kids

great *great* *great* *great*

food *food* *food* *food* *food*

great food

truck *truck truck truck*

car *car car car car car*

truck and car

cute *cute* *cute* *cute* *cute*

fun *fun* *fun* *fun* *fun*

nice nice nice nice nice

candy candy candy

nice and candy

mom *mom* *mom* *mom*

dady *dady* *dady* *dady*

mom and dady

best _best_ _best_ _best_ _best_

good _good_ _good_ _good_

best and good

what   what   what   what

who   who   who   who

each   each   each   each   each

tree   tree   tree   tree   tree

each and tree

farm farm farm farm

sky sky sky sky sky

farm and sky

lunch lunch lunch lunch

dinner dinner dinner

lunch and dinner

class class class class

family family family

class and family

ground   ground   ground

heard   heard   heard   heard

ground and heard

guice *guice* *guice* *guice*

merry *merry* *merry*

guice and merry

orange *orange* *orange*

apple *apple* *apple* *apple*

Picture   Picture   Picture

Queen   Queen   Queen   Queen

picture and queen

Running   Running

Shield   Shield   Shield

Teacher   Teacher   Teacher
Student   Student   Student
teacher and student

Brother *Brother* *Brother*

Sister *Sister* *Sister* *Sister*

brother and sister

Part 3:
Learning Numbers

Trace the numbers and practice writing them in the remaining space!

Use the blank practice page to write on your own at the end.

1 1 1 1 1 1 1 1 1

1 1 1 1 1 1 1 1 1

One One One One

One One One One

2 2 2 2 2 2 2 2

2 2 2 2 2 2 2 2

Two Two Two Two

Two Two Two Two

3 3 3 3 3 3 3 3

3 3 3 3 3 3 3 3

Three Three Three Three

Three Three Three Three

4   4   4   4   4   4   4   4

4   4   4   4   4   4   4   4

Four   Four   Four   Four

Four   Four   Four   Four

5 5 5 5 5 5 5 5

5 5 5 5 5 5 5 5

Five Five Five Five

Five Five Five Five

6　6　6　6　6　6　6　6

6　6　6　6　6　6　6　6

Six　Six　Six　Six　Six

Six　Six　Six　Six　Six

7 7 7 7 7 7 7 7

7 7 7 7 7 7 7 7

Seven Seven Seven

Seven Seven Seven

8   8   8   8   8   8   8   8

8   8   8   8   8   8   8   8

Eight   Eight   Eight

Eight   Eight   Eight

9 9 9 9 9 9 9 9

9 9 9 9 9 9 9 9

Nine Nine Nine

Nine Nine Nine

10 10 10 10 10 10

10 10 10 10 10 10

Ten Ten Ten Ten Ten

Ten Ten Ten Ten Ten

GREAT
You did it!

A
A
alligator

B
bear
B

cat

D
duck
D
D D D D D
D D D D D

elephant

flamingo

G
giraffe

horse

iguana

jaguar

K
koala
K

L

lama

monkey

numbat

owl

P

penguin

P

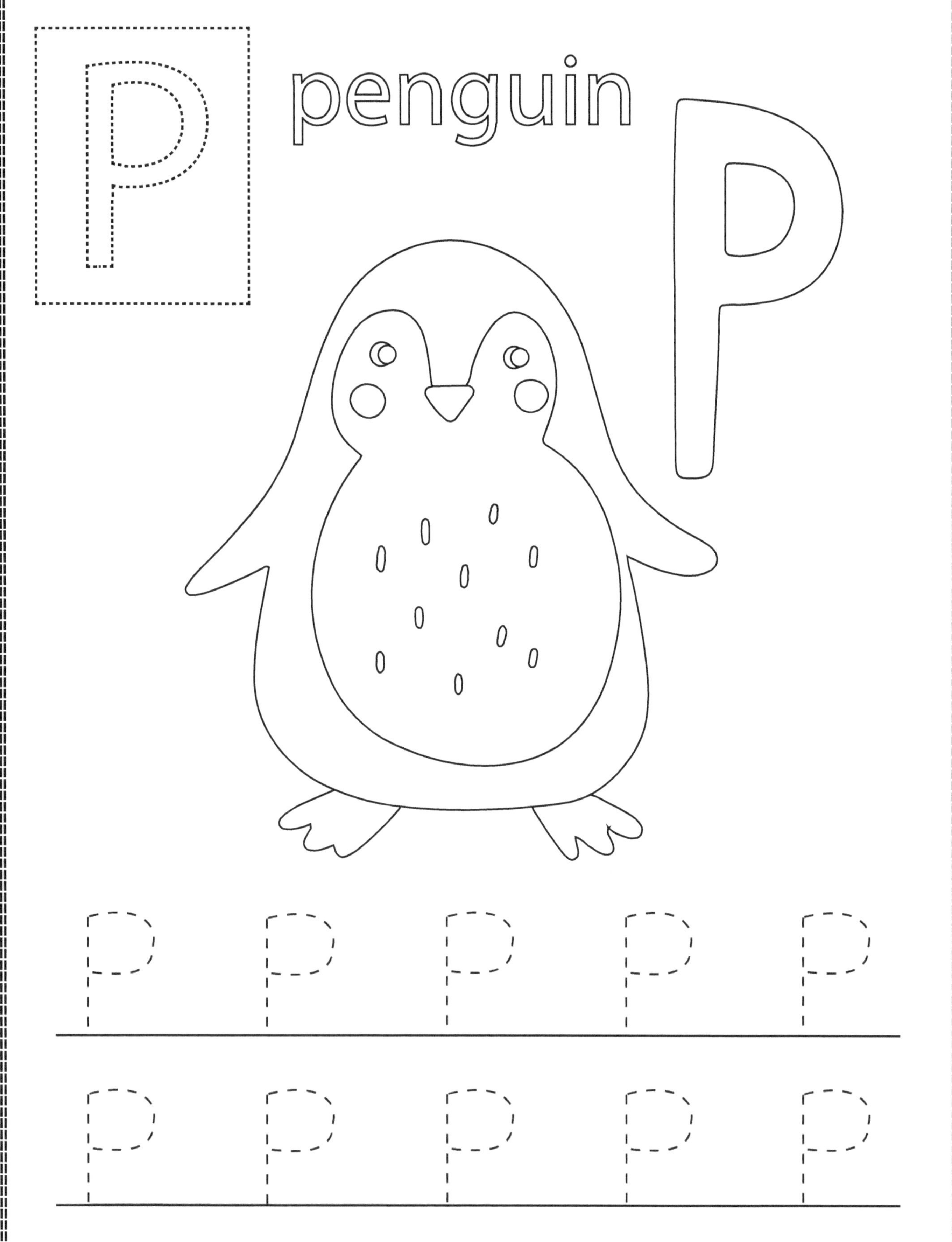

P P P P P

P P P P P

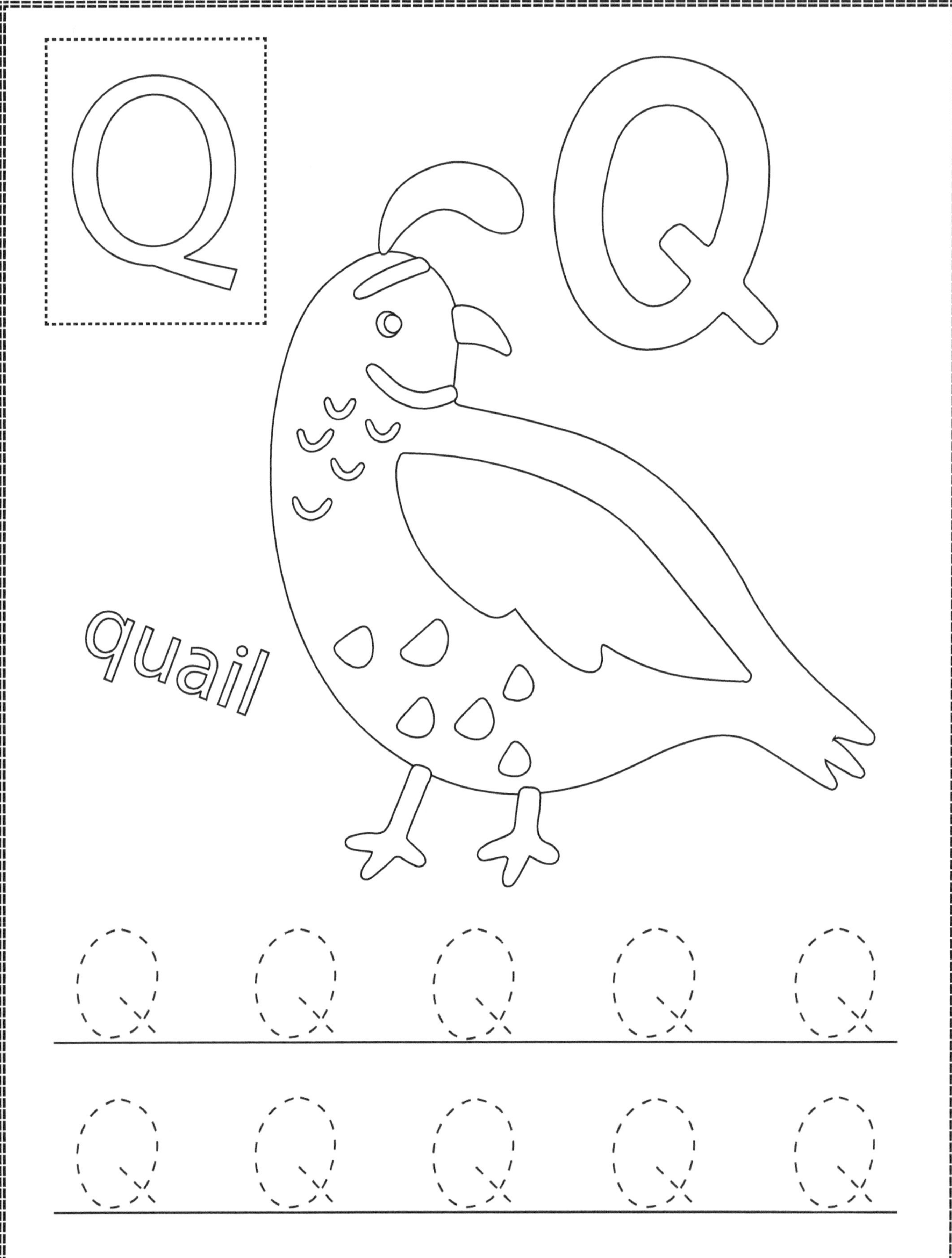
Q
Q
quail

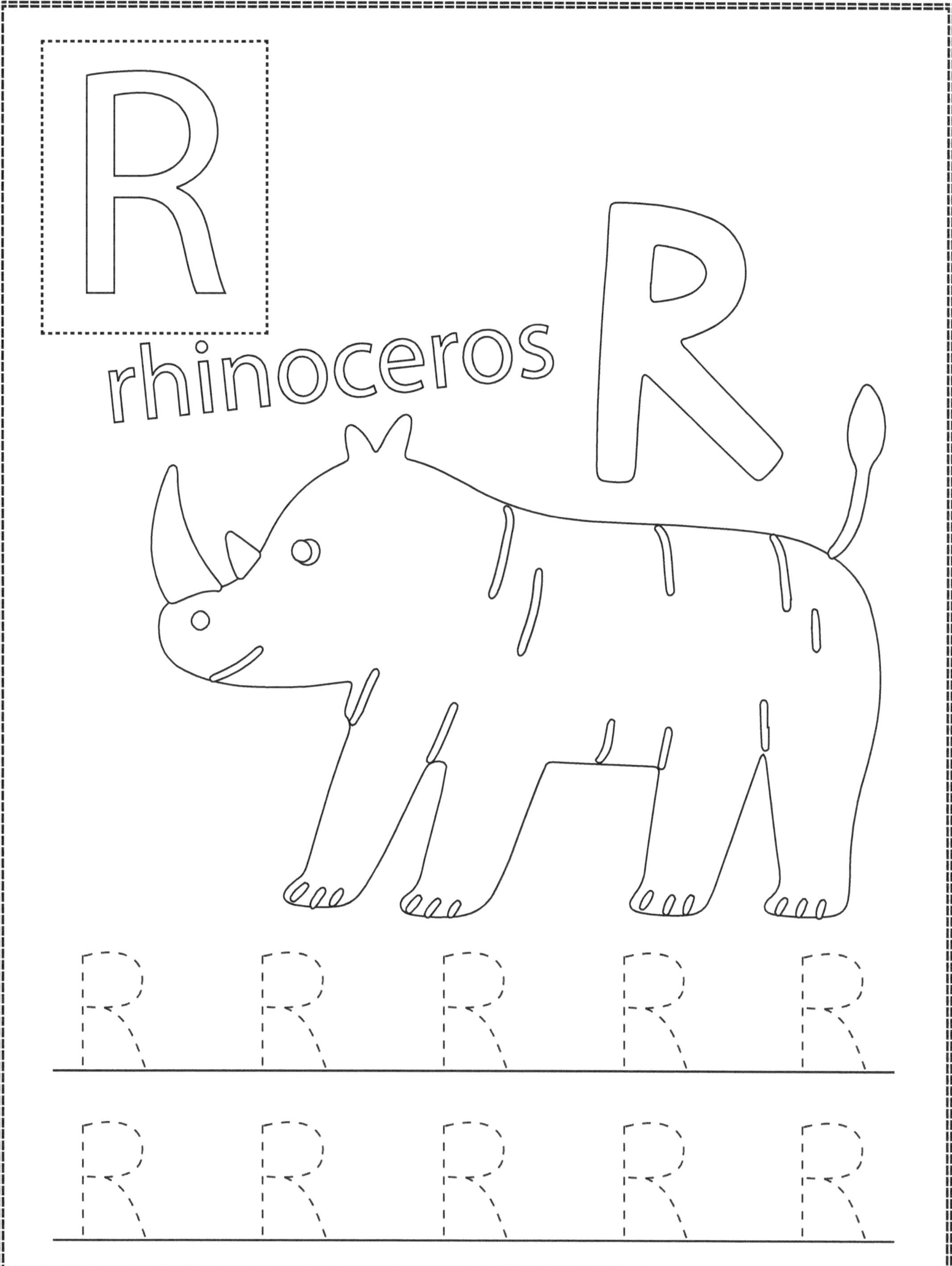

R
rhinoceros
R
R R R R R
R R R R R

sheep

T
tiger
T
T

U
unicorn
U

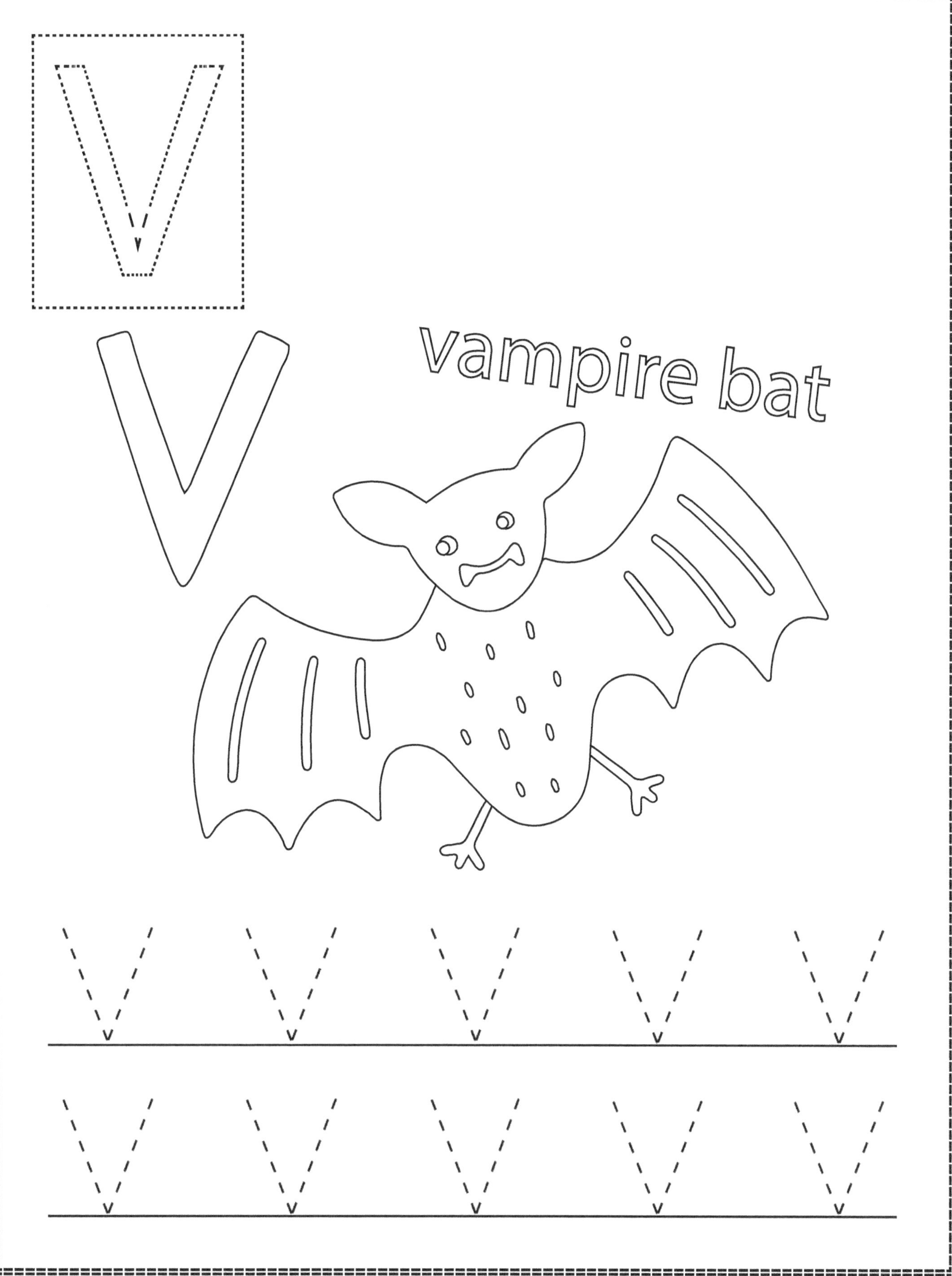

vampire bat

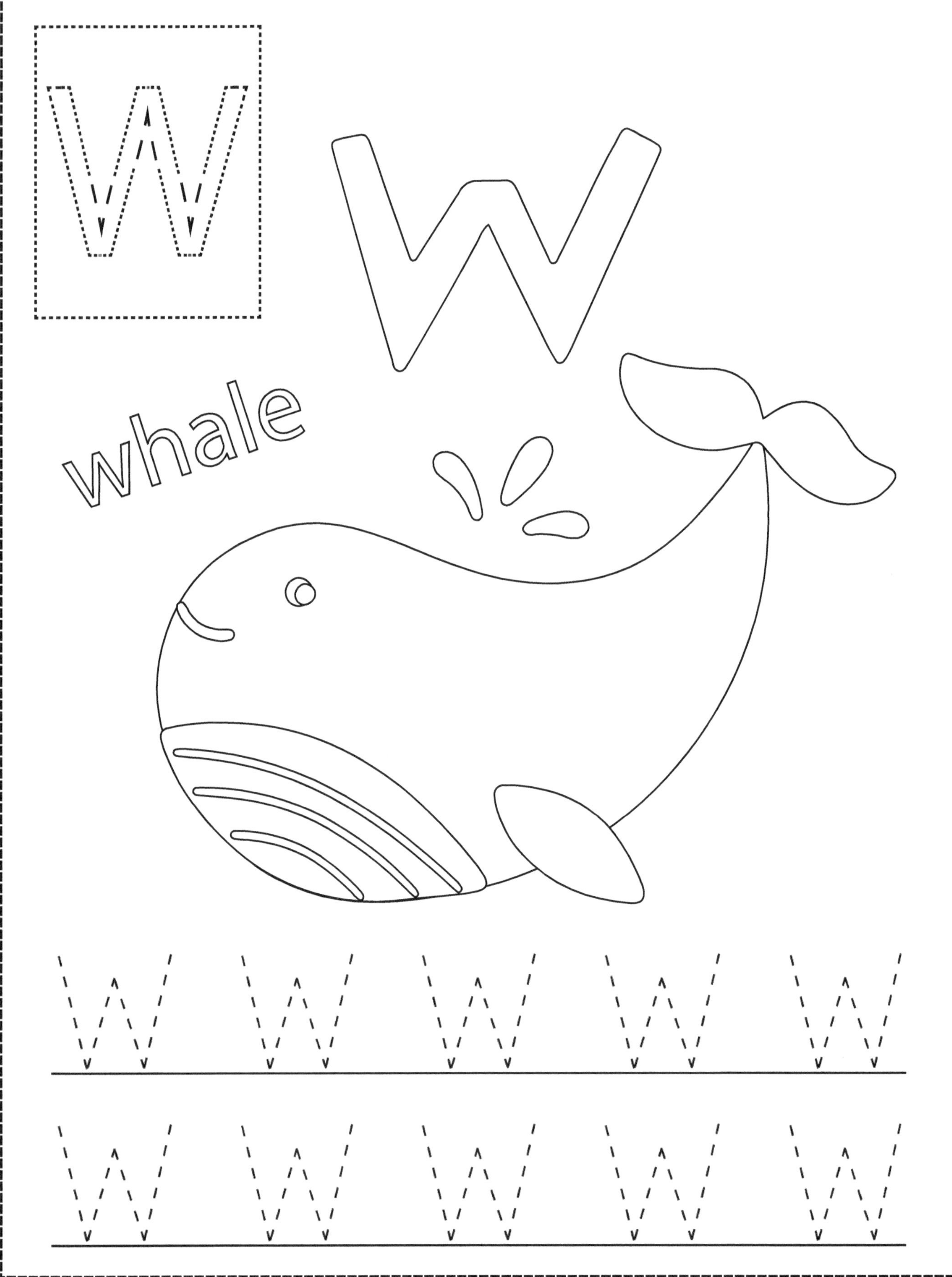

W
whale

xerus

Y
Yak
Y

Z z
zebra